Material Matters

States of Matter

Carol Baldwin

Raintree

Chicago, Illinois

For information, address the publisher:
Raintree, 100 N. LaSalle, Suite 1200, Chicago, IL 60602

Printed and bound in China
08 07 06
10 9 8 7 6 5 4 3 2

Library of Congress Cataloging-in-Publication Data

Baldwin, Carol, 1943-
  States of matter / Carol Baldwin.
    p. cm. -- (Material matters)
Contents: What is matter? -- Solids -- Liquids -- Gases -- Plasmas --
Changes in state -- Fluids in action -- Weird water.
  ISBN 1-4109-0553-5 (lib. bdg. : hardcover), 1-4109-0940-9 (Pbk.)
  1. Matter--Properties--Juvenile literature. [1. Matter--Properties.]
I. Title. II. Series: Baldwin, Carol, 1943-   Material matters.
  QC173.36.B33 2004
  530.4--dc21
                              2003008293

Acknowledgments
The publisher would like to thank the following for permission to reproduce photographs:
P. 4 Science Photo Library; pp. 4–5 Robert Harding Picture Library; p. 5 (top) Corbis; p. 5 (middle) M. Peters/Art Directors & Trip; p. 5 (bottom) Corbis; p. 6 M. Newman/FLPA; pp. 6–7 Simon Lewis/Science Photo Library; pp. 7, 8, 18, 21, 22–23, 24, 35, 38 (right) Trevor Clifford; pp. 8–9 B. Turner/Art Directors & Trip; p. 9 S. Fraser/Science Photo Library; p. 10 Mark E. Gibson/Corbis; pp. 10–11 Richard T. Nowitz/Corbis; pp. 11, 12 (left) D. Boone/Corbis; p. 12 (right) M. Land/Science Photo Library; p. 13 Sheila Terry/Science Photo Library; p. 14 J. Ellard/Art Directors & Trip; pp. 14–15 Lindsay Hebberd/Corbis; p. 15 Sandy Felsenthal/Corbis; p. 16 Charles D. Winter/Science Photo Library; pp. 16–17 M. Thomas/FLPA; p. 17 C. Sneddon/Anthony Blake Picture Library; pp. 18–19 R. Drury/Art Directors & Trip; p. 19 Comstock; p. 20 Roger Ball/Corbis; pp. 20–21, 45 TRL Ltd/Science Photo Library; p. 22 H. Rogers/Art Directors & Trip; p. 23 Shout Pictures; pp. 24–25 C. Claughton/The Skyscan Photolibrary; R. Francis/Robert Harding Picture Library; p. 26 Digital Vision; pp. 26–27 Corbis; p. 27 John Cleare Mountain Photography; p. 28 M. Burnett/Science Photo Library; p. 29 Corbis; p. 30 Corbis; pp. 30–31 Hubble Space Telescope Center/NASA; p. 31 Douglas Mesney/Corbis; p. 32 P. Pebbles/Robert Harding Picture Library; pp. 32–33 M. Peters/Art Directors & Trip; p. 33 David Stoecklein/Corbis; p. 34 F. Blackburn/Art Directors & Trip; pp. 34–35 T. Craddock/Science Photo Library; p. 36 Jeffrey L. Rotman/Corbis; pp. 36–37 Corbis; p. 38 (left) Ted Streshinsky/Corbis; p. 39 Bettmann/Corbis; p. 40 By Silvestris/FLPA; pp. 40–41 Corbis; p. 41 Minden Pictures/FLPA; p. 42 J. Bastable/FLPA; pp. 42–43 Lee Frost/Robert Harding Picture Library; p. 43 Corbis; p. 44 Richard T. Nowitz/Corbis.

Cover photograph of a plasma globe reproduced with permission of Alfred Pasieka/Science Photo Library.

Contents

Some words are shown in bold, **like this.** You can find out what they mean by looking in the glossary. You can also look out for them in the Word Bank at the bottom of each page.

Up, Up, and Away

Flying farmyard

The Montgolfier brothers in France made the first hot-air balloons in 1782. Their first balloon was made of cloth and paper. It carried no passengers. However, a balloon that flew on September 19, 1783, did carry passengers. They were a duck, a rooster, and a sheep.

The balloon fills with hot air as the burner roars to life. The ground crew hold the balloon down until the pilot climbs into the basket. They let go of the ropes. The balloon rises up into the air. The balloon pilot turns off the burner. The balloon floats silently through the air in the gentle wind. It drifts for several miles. Then it heads straight toward a hill. The pilot turns on the burner again and the balloon rises. It safely clears the hill. He turns off the burner and the balloon slowly starts to drop lower.

The balloon took off in Paris, lifted by an on-board stove burning wool and straw.

Word Bank

deflate   to let air or gas out of something
freeze   to change from a liquid to a solid

Back on the ground

The balloon touches down in a large field. The ground crew have been following it in a truck. They rush to the balloon and grab ropes attached to the basket. They hold the ropes tightly so the balloon will not be caught by the wind as it **deflates.** Otherwise it might be dragged along the ground with the basket bumping all the way.

Why does the balloon rise when the burner is turned on? What makes it come back down to the ground? To understand how a hot-air balloon works, you need to know something about solids, liquids, and gases. These are all **states of matter.**

Balloning started as a sport in the 1960s in the United States and Britain. The sport spread to Australia in the 1970s. Today, hot-air balloons compete in events all over the world.

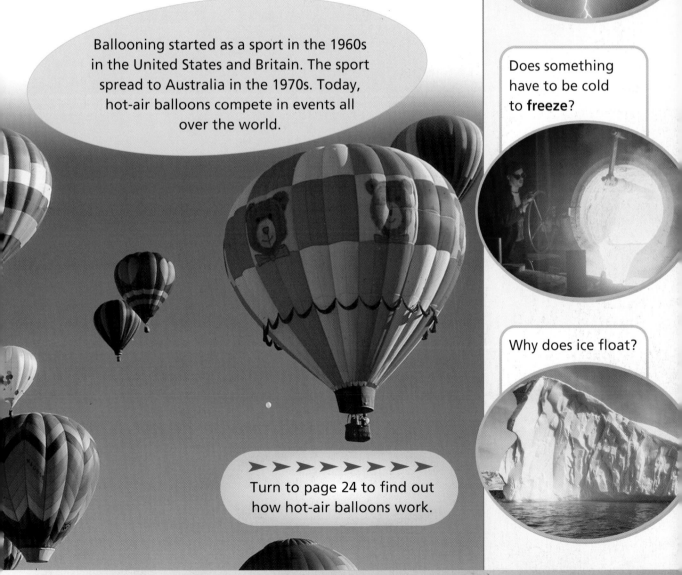

>>>>>>>>>> Turn to page 24 to find out how hot-air balloons work.

Find out later...

How hot is a lightning bolt?

Does something have to be cold to **freeze**?

Why does ice float?

matter   anything that takes up space and has weight
state of matter   whether something is solid, liquid, or gas

What Is Matter?

Tiny particles

This sand sculpture has mass and takes up space. However, it is made of small grains of sand. In a similar way, each grain of sand is made of much smaller particles of matter. These tiny particles are made of silicon and oxygen **atoms** that are joined together.

Matter is anything that takes up space. Matter includes everything from a speck of dust to a huge ocean. Matter is everywhere. Water, air, food, buildings, plants, animals, and people all take up space, so they are made of matter.

Mass

Matter is made of tiny **particles** called atoms that are much too small to see. Besides taking up space, these particles also have **mass.** Mass is the amount of matter in an object. The mass of an object is measured in grams or kilograms.

Volume

The amount of space an object takes up is its **volume.**

The metal of this building has mass and takes up space. So do the worker, the torch, and the air. They are all types of matter.

Word Bank   atom   smallest particle of an element
particle   small part of something

Properties of matter

Matter can be described in two main ways. It has physical **properties** and chemical properties. Some physical properties are color, shape, hardness, and state of matter. You can tell what the physical properties of something are by examining it. You can only tell what its chemical properties are when it reacts with something else. The ability of wood to burn is a chemical **property**.

Density

All substances also have the physical property of **density**. Density tells us how much mass is in a particular volume of matter. Bricks have a much higher density than foam packing material. It would be harder to lift a box filled with bricks than a box filled with packing material. However, both boxes take up the same amount of space, so they have the same volume.

Would you drink this glass of liquid?

If we have a liquid and we are not sure if it is water, we can compare its properties to water. Ice cubes float in water. The ice cubes in this photo have sunk, so the liquid cannot be water. In fact, the liquid is rubbing alcohol.

property feature of something

Thermostats

Inside a thermostat is a bar made of two metal strips joined to each other. One strip is made of brass and the other is iron.

As the temperature changes, the bar bends. This is because brass expands faster than iron.

These metal strips are used in thermostats that control central heating. A change in temperature makes the strip bend and turn the heating on or off.

Matter and energy

Matter exists in different forms. Most matter can be solid, liquid, or gas. These forms are called the **states of matter.** The way the **atoms** are arranged in each state is different. It changes with the amount of energy available to the matter.

Turn to page 30 to find out about a fourth state of matter.

Thermal expansion

Heat causes solid objects to **expand,** or get bigger. These solid objects **contract,** or get smaller, when they cool. An object expands when the tiny **particles,** or atoms, that make up the object move further apart. An object contracts because its atoms move closer together. The atoms do not change size when an object expands or contracts. Very cold weather can sometimes snap electrical wires. The wires become so tight as they contract that they break.

Heat also causes liquids and gases to expand in the same way. But not all materials expand and contract by the same amount.

Bridges are built with a space between the bridge and the roadbed. When the weather is cold, the gap between the bridge and roadbed is wide. On warm days, the metal of the bridge expands and the gap is narrow. Without the gap the bridge could expand so much that it would bend and crack in hot weather.

Word Bank   geothermal energy   heat from deep inside the earth
geyser   vent that shoots up water and steam from underground

Changing state

Matter can change from one state to another when energy is added or taken away. Usually, this energy is in the form of heat. When an ice cube is heated, it changes from ice to water. So heat changes a solid to a liquid. If the water is heated, it will become a gas. So heat changes a liquid to a gas.

Whether it is ice, liquid water, or **water vapor,** the substance is still water. If a substance can change state, this is a physical **property.** When a substance changes state this is a **physical change.**

▶▶▶▶▶▶▶▶▶▶▶▶

Turn to page 33 to find out what happens when a solid changes to a liquid.

There she blows

Heat from deep inside the Earth is called **geothermal energy.** In some places, this energy heats water underground. If it is heated enough, it will change state. Then hot water and steam can shoot out in a **geyser.**

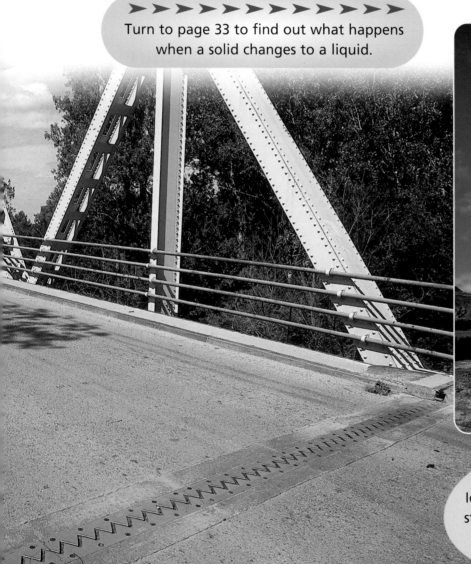

The Strokkur geyser in Iceland shoots a column of steam and super-hot water 100 feet (30 meters) into the air.

physical change   change in the way something looks, not in what makes it up
water vapor   water in gas state

Solids

The solid parts of this fish kept their shape and volume when they were buried.

Fossils

Fossils are what remains of plants and animals that lived millions of years ago. When this fish died, its body was quickly covered up by sand on the bottom of a lake. The solid, hard parts, like the bones, gradually turned into rock over thousands of years.

A solid is a **state of matter** that has a definite shape and **volume.** That means that a solid keeps its shape and does not need a container to hold it. A solid also has a definite volume, which means that it takes up the same amount of space wherever you put it. Wood, pencils, coins, and nails are all solids.

How atoms are arranged and move

Atoms are tightly packed together in a solid. The atoms in a solid cannot easily be pushed aside. They cannot change position easily. The atoms can only vibrate back and forth in the same place. That is why it is impossible to walk through something like a brick wall or a wooden door.

A block of ice has a definite shape and volume. Artists can only make ice sculptures by chipping or sawing away chunks of solid ice.

Word Bank   conduction   transfer of heat or electricity from one particle to another in a solid
                                    conductor   material through which heat or electricity pass easily

Some other properties of solids

- Heat travels through solids by a process called **conduction.** Heat energy passes from atom to atom in conduction.
- Some solids are good **conductors** of heat and electricity. That is why copper is used in home wiring and to make some pots and pans.
- Other solids are poor conductors of heat and electricity. That is why plastics are used to **insulate** wires and as handles on pots and pans.
- Some solids, like gold, can be stretched into wires or hammered into sheets. Others, like glass, cannot.
- Some solids, like wood, will float in water and others, like stone, will sink.

Fast Fact

In the world around us, there are many more different solids than there are liquids or gases.

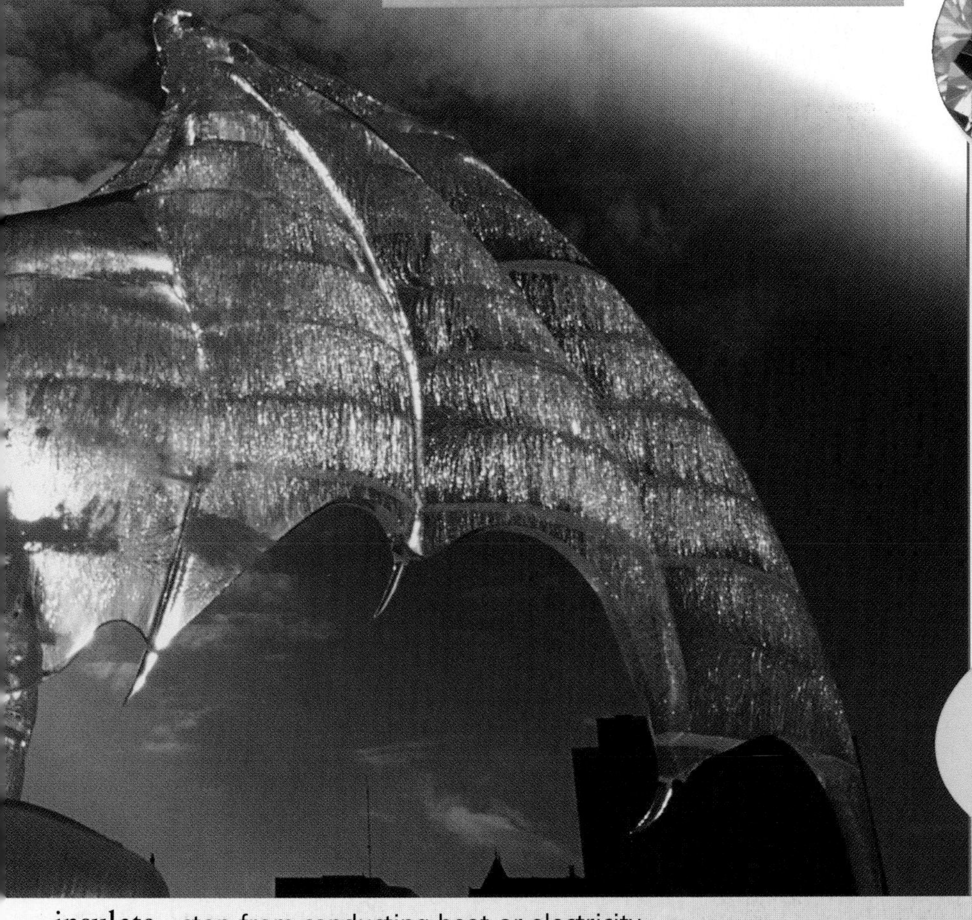

Forms of carbon

Graphite in pencils is a form of carbon. Diamond is another form of carbon. Graphite and diamonds are so different because of the different ways carbon atoms join together. In graphite the carbon atoms are joined in sheets. In a diamond, each carbon atom is tightly joined to other carbon atoms all around it.

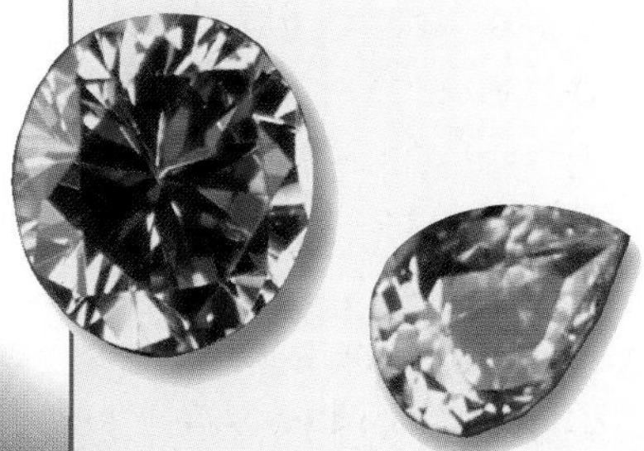

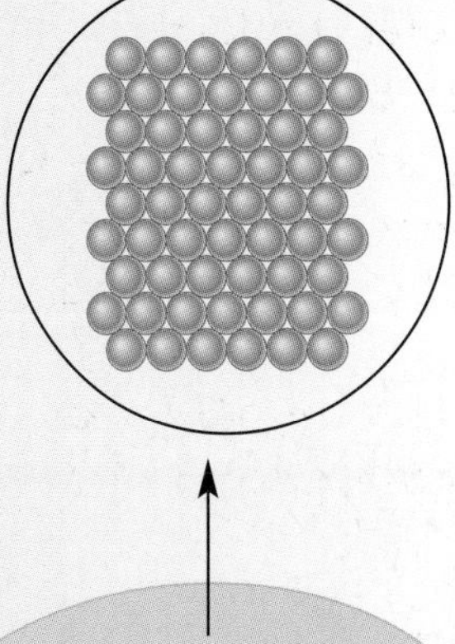

This diagram shows one way that atoms can pack closely together in a solid.

insulate stop from conducting heat or electricity

Diamonds

Diamonds are crystals that have six or eight sides. Crystals have definite surfaces, or faces, that are smooth. They break neatly along these surfaces. Diamond cutters make use of these crystal faces when they cut diamonds for jewelry.

Crystalline solids

Most solids form **crystals.** In crystals, **particles** are arranged in repeating patterns. There are seven basic crystal shapes. All have straight edges and smooth surfaces. When you break a crystal, a flat surface is left. Salt, snowflakes, and diamonds are crystals. Different kinds of solid have crystals of different shapes. Salt and diamonds both form cube-shaped crystals. But snowflakes form hexagonal or six-sided crystals.

Most crystals form when a **melted** substance cools. The size of the crystals depends on how quickly the substance cools. If the substance cools slowly, a large crystal may form. If the substance cools quickly, many small crystals may form. Gems that are used in jewelry, such as diamonds or rubies, consist of a single, large crystal.

amorphous   solid in which particles are not arranged in an orderly pattern
crystal   solid in which particles are arranged in an orderly pattern

Amorphous solids

A few solids have a different pattern of particles. The particles do not form regular, repeating patterns. These materials are called **amorphous solids.** Amorphous means without form. Chocolate, butter, rubber bands, and glass are examples. Broken glass has curved surfaces, not flat ones. Some amorphous solids form naturally, for example, obsidian. Unlike crystals, which melt suddenly at a given temperature, amorphous solids melt gradually. Candle wax, for instance, gets slowly softer and softer as it melts.

Fast Fact
Some of the rocks on the moon are glassy, amorphous solids. They probably formed after **meteorites** hit the moon. The crashes melted some of the moon's surface. The melted materials cooled too quickly for crystals to form.

Obsidian
Obsidian is a kind of natural glass. It forms when **lava** from a volcano cools too quickly for crystals to form. Obsidian breaks into curved, clean surfaces with round-shaped ripples. The broken pieces of obsidian have very sharp edges.

Quartz crystals can be colorless, pink, purple, yellow, or brown. But all quartz crystals have the same shape.

In ancient times, some people made cutting tools and arrowheads from obsidian. They did this by chipping away the outer edge of a piece of obsidian using a deer antler and a small stone. Obsidian blades have the sharpest cutting edges known. Today some hospitals even use obsidian blades when performing heart surgery.

lava molten rock that has risen to the earth's surface
meteorite lump of space rock or metal that has crashed into a planet

Solids around us

Solids are everywhere. They are used for building everything
from microchips to skyscrapers. Their huge range of
properties means there is a solid **suitable** for every job.

Steel

Steel is iron with small amounts of carbon and other
substances in it. Steel is used to make objects as large as
oil tankers and as small as nuts and bolts. Different kinds
of steel are used for different purposes because they have
different properties. Low-carbon steel is used for car bodies.
Stronger medium-carbon steel is used for making ships and
beams for buildings. High-carbon steel is very strong
but difficult to shape. It is used in railroad tracks.

Stainless steel contains a metal called chromium.
It does not rust, so it is used to make equipment
for hospitals and kitchens.

Steel-framed homes are
safer in fires, earthquakes,
and high winds. They are
also safe from wood-eating
insects like termites.

The Red Fort in Delhi, India,
was built in the 1600s from
solid red sandstone.

composites   material designed by combining other materials
recycled   treated so that the material can be used again

Nickel steel does not stretch easily, so it is used in bridge cables. Suspension bridges are held up by cables. They are very strong, thick ropes made using hundreds of steel wires. The floors of bridges are made from steel plates or from concrete with steel rods in it. Steel beams and columns are used to support the bridge.

Rocks

Hard rocks like granite and sandstone are good building materials for houses and walls. Slate is used for roofs and floors in many homes. Even soft rocks are useful. Heating clay or **shale** with crushed limestone makes cement. It is used for making concrete and laying bricks. Bricks are made by baking shaped clay.

These car body panels are made from composite materials.

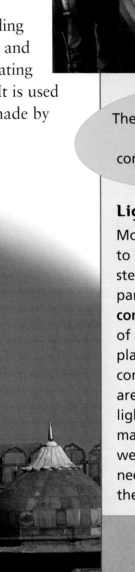

Lighter cars

Most car bodies used to be made from steel. Now, many car parts are made from **composites.** Fibers of glass are put into plastic to make composites. They are strong but lightweight. Cars made with composites weigh less, so they need less fuel to move them along.

shale   rock formed from clay or mud in thin layers
suitable   right for the job

Liquids

A dangerous liquid

Mercury is the only metal that is a liquid at room temperature. It has been used in thermometers, electrical switches, tooth fillings, and batteries. However, it is unusual to find mercury in things around the home now, because it is a poison.

Liquids do not have a definite shape. When milk is in a carton, it takes the shape of the carton. But if it is poured into a glass, it takes the shape of the glass. However, a liquid does have a definite **volume**. A quart of milk will take up a quart of space in a glass or spilled on the floor.

How particles are arranged and move

A liquid like water has **atoms** that are close together. But the atoms are not quite as close together as they are in a solid. The atoms can move around one another more easily, so a liquid can flow. That is why orange juice can be poured from a bottle into a glass. That is also why a person can wade or swim through water.

Water in a stream takes the shape of the stream. When it flows into a lake, it takes the shape of the lake.

Word Bank   convection   flow of heat due to the rise of hotter matter in liquid or gas
surface tension   force that pulls atoms of a liquid together at its surface

Some other properties of liquids

- Heat makes liquids **expand**.
- Heat spreads through liquids by a process called **convection**. When a pot of water is heated on a stove, the water at the bottom of the pot is heated first. The heated water is less dense, so it rises. Colder water from above sinks to take its place. This movement spreads the heat throughout the water.
- It is very hard to squeeze liquids into a smaller volume or stretch them out to fill a larger volume.
- **Surface tension** makes the surface of a liquid act like the tight, stretchy skin of a balloon. This is why a glass can be filled so full that the water bulges above the rim of the glass.

▶▶▶▶▶▶▶▶▶▶▶▶
Turn to page 38 to find how the **property** of being hard to squeeze is used.

Go with the flow

Liquids like water are easy to pour. Others, like honey, pour more slowly. Tar is almost impossible to pour. **Viscosity** is the word that describes how a liquid flows or pours. Water has a low viscosity. It flows quickly. Honey has a high viscosity. It flows slowly.

Liquids get less viscous as they are heated.

Atoms can move around each other more easily in a liquid.

viscosity   how easily a liquid flows or pours

Motor oil

Motor oil lubricates the moving parts of an engine. Every can of motor oil is labeled with its **viscosity** grade. Oil with a lower number flows more easily. It is better for cold-weather driving.

Oil with a higher number flows more slowly and is better for hot-weather driving.

Liquids around us

Water is the most common liquid on the earth. But other liquids play an important part in our lives.

Oil and its products

Crude oil is a dark, thick liquid found deep underground. People drill oil wells to get the oil out of the ground. Oil refineries separate the different parts of crude oil. Gasoline, paraffin, diesel fuel, fuel oil, and **lubricating** oils all come from crude oil.

Large trucks, as well as some tractors and cars, use diesel fuel to run their engines.

acid   chemical that contains hydrogen and has a pH of less than 7
digest   to break down food so it can be used by the body

Without oil, our everyday lives would grind to a halt. Oil is needed to make fuels that run cars, trucks, trains, ships, and airplanes. Some power stations burn oil to make electricity. And some homes use oil burners for heating. Lubricating oils help machine parts slide past each other easily so that the machines work well.

Other liquids

Familiar liquids include foods such as milk, juices, honey, cooking oil, and soft drinks. Other liquids around the home might include liquid soaps, paints, and rubbing alcohol. **Acids,** such as vinegar, are another group of important liquids. Many foods, such as lemons, tomatoes, apples, oranges, and pickles, contain acids.

Sulfuric acid and hydrochloric acid are important to many industries. These acids are used to treat metals. Iron parts are dipped in acid to remove rust. Sulfuric acid is also used in car batteries and for making fertilizers. Hydrochloric acid is also found in our stomachs. It helps **digest** food there.

In a normal thermometer, colored alcohol rises in a narrow tube as the liquid gets hotter and **expands**. The level falls as the liquid gets colder and contracts.

Fast Fact
"Heartburn" is caused when hydrochloric acid in the stomach backs up into the **esophagus**.

lubricate   to make slippery; reduce friction
esophagus   pipe from the mouth to the stomach

Gases

Portable air

Gas can be squeezed so that a lot of it will fit into a small space. This allows scuba divers to carry enough air in one tank to breathe for an hour underwater. Firefighters also breathe from tanks of **compressed** air when they enter burning buildings.

Firefighters breathe compressed air to protect themselves from thick, toxic smoke.

Gas is a **state of matter** with no definite shape. Gases take the shape of whatever container they are put into. Air has different shapes in a basketball and in a bicycle tire. Gases have no definite **volume,** either. The **particles** of a gas spread out to take up all the space available. Any container of a gas is always completely full.

How particles are arranged and move

Particles in a gas are much farther apart than particles in a liquid. Gas particles also move around constantly. As the particles move around, they bounce off one another and off the walls of their container. If two gases are put together they will **diffuse** and mix with one another. Diffusion is the reason smells spread quickly through the air.

Fast Facts

- Particles of oxygen gas in air at 70 °F (20 °C) have an average speed of about 1,100 miles per hour (1,700 kilometers per hour).
- The natural gas used in many stoves and fires is **odorless**. But chemicals that do have smells are mixed with it. If there is a gas leak, the **odor** will spread throughout the room. This will alert people to leave the building.

Word Bank   compress   squeeze into a smaller space
diffuse   how particles of a gas spread evenly through another gas

Heating gases

Heat travels through gases the same way it travels through liquids. Hot air above a heater rises. Cold air flows in to take its place, becomes hot and also rises. A circular current of air moves around a room, carrying heat with it. When heat travels in this way, it is called **convection**.

The gas released into these air bags quickly spreads out to fill the entire volume of the bag. The gas also takes the shape of the air bags.

You can spray air freshener in one corner and smell it a few minutes later across the room.

Spray cans contain gases that have been squeezed into small spaces. When the valve is pressed, the gas **expands**. It pushes tiny liquid particles out into the air in the room. These liquid particles change to gases. The gases spread throughout the room.

odor smell
odorless without any smell

Barometer

A barometer measures changes in the pressure of the air around us. These changes help to predict future weather. Inside this barometer is a chamber from which most of the air has been removed. The chamber has an arrow hooked to it.

Behavior of gases

If you squeeze a balloon filled with gas, the gas inside pushes back. The gas pushes on the inside of the balloon. The total **force** depends on the **area** of the balloon's surface. The amount of force per unit area is called **pressure**. The pressure is the total force divided by the area of the surface.

Moving gas **particles** exert force when they collide with other particles or the walls of their containers. Gas pressure results from billions of collisions of gas particles on an object. If a certain number of gas particles are put into a large container, the particles will spread out. But if the same number of gas particles are squeezed into a tiny container, the particles will be packed closer together.

When air pressure is high, more air particles push on the sides of the chamber and the arrow points to a higher number on the front of the barometer. This means the weather will be fair.

area   amount of surface
force   push or pull

Volume and pressure

When gas particles are far apart, fewer of them hit the walls of their container. So the pressure they exert is small. When the gas is **compressed,** the particles are pushed closer together. When the particles are closer together, they hit the container walls and each other more often. So they exert greater pressure. In other words, if the **volume** of a gas increases, its pressure decreases. And if the volume of the same amount of a gas decreases, its pressure increases. This is true only if the temperature of the gas stays the same.

If the air pressure in a bicycle tire is too low, more air can be pumped in. The more particles of air that are pumped into the tire, the higher the pressure gets. The pressure of the gas particles bouncing off the inside of the bicycle tire keep the tire **inflated.**

Putting out fires

Some fire extinguishers have a cartridge of carbon dioxide inside. The carbon dioxide is under high pressure and is in its liquid state. When the handle is pressed, some liquid is released. It changes back into a gas at normal pressure. A small volume of liquid becomes a large volume of gas.

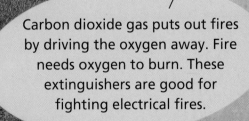

Carbon dioxide gas puts out fires by driving the oxygen away. Fire needs oxygen to burn. These extinguishers are good for fighting electrical fires.

pressure   force divided by the area it presses on

Volume and temperature

If a balloon is blown up and tied closed, air is held inside it. If the balloon is put into very cold water, it will **contract.** If the balloon is then pushed into hot water or held over a heater, the balloon will **expand.**

There is a relationship between the **volume** and temperature of a gas. It describes what happens to a gas in a **flexible** container, such as a balloon. When energy (heat) is added to a gas, its temperature increases. The added energy also causes the **particles** to move faster and hit the walls of the balloon more often. Since the balloon can stretch, the gas pushes the walls of the balloon out. The volume of the gas increases and makes the balloon bigger.

Checking tire pressure

When the air temperature changes, people check their tire pressure. Tires are flexible containers, so when the temperature goes down, so does the volume of the air inside the tire. In very cold weather, tires may become flattened on the bottom. This is dangerous.

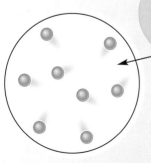

Atoms in a gas move around freely and fill all the available space, pushing against the sides of the container.

Word Bank   flexible   able to stretch or bend

Inflating hot-air balloons

The burner flame in a hot-air balloon heats the air inside the balloon. As the air is heated, it expands and the balloon **inflates.** When the burner is turned off, the air in the balloon cools and contracts.

Temperature and pressure

There is a relationship between the temperature and **pressure** of a gas. It describes what happens to a gas in a container such as a metal tank. A metal tank is not flexible like a balloon. In a closed tank, the volume of the gas cannot change. But when the gas is heated, its particles gain energy. The particles bounce against the container's walls more often and with greater **force.** This results in higher pressure. If the gas is cooled, the particles move more slowly and the pressure drops.

Scuba tanks

The air in a scuba tank is under more than 200 times normal air pressure. Filled scuba tanks should never be left in a hot car. The heat could make the pressure inside rise so much that the tanks explode.

Hot-air balloons make use of the behavior of gases every time they launch. As the temperature of the hot air increases, the volume of the balloon also increases.

A display shows divers how much air they have left.

inflate   to force gas or air into an object

Water vapor in the air

The amount of **water vapor** in the air changes from day to day and place to place. In the Sahara Desert, the air feels hot and dry. In a tropical rain forest, the air feels hot and damp. We say this air is **humid**.

There is so much water vapor in rain forest air that it looks misty.

The earth's atmosphere

Air is all around us. We do not usually notice the air unless it is a windy day or we cycle quickly down a hill. But without it, life on the earth would be impossible.

Gases in the air

The layer of gases that surround the earth is called the **atmosphere.** It contains all the gases living things need. It also protects living things from the Sun's harmful rays. The atmosphere contains many gases, but two of them make up most of the air. There is more nitrogen in air than any other gas. It makes up 78 percent of the air. Oxygen is the gas needed by all living things. It makes up 21 percent of the air. Other gases make up one percent of the air.

Oxygen 21% — Other gases 1%

Nitrogen 78%

The main gases in air.

Word Bank   altitude   distance above the ocean (sea level)
atmosphere   layer of gases that surrounds a planet like Earth

Air pressure and altitude

The gases in air are made of **matter,** so they have **mass.**
The mass of air causes air **pressure.** At sea level, the
force of the air on every square foot of the earth's
surface is equal to the weight of a large truck. Why
doesn't this pressure crush living things? Because the
liquids and gases inside living things create a pressure
that is equal to the air outside.

Air pressure changes with **altitude.** The higher we go up
a mountain, the lower the air pressure becomes. That
is because there is less air above us to push down. High
in the mountains, the air is thinner and there is less
oxygen in it. This makes it hard to breathe.

Climbing Mount Everest

Above 8,200 feet (2,500
meters), climbers can
suffer from altitude
sickness. It happens
when they climb too
high too quickly. The air
thins and all the oxygen
a climber takes in goes
into the work of just
breathing. Climbers can
get weak and have
accidents. Most
mountain climbers
breathe from a tank of
oxygen to avoid this.

Fast Fact
The total weight of the
Earth's atmosphere is
about 500 trillion tons.

The atmosphere is all
around us, yet most of
the time we do not
notice it.

humid   moist or damp

Giant balloons

Scientists send giant balloons filled with **helium** gas into the stratosphere to learn more about this layer. As a balloon rises through the atmosphere, the **pressure** on the outside of the balloon decreases. This lets the balloon **expand**. The weather balloon's **volume** can increase more than 250 times as it rises to the stratosphere.

Balloons carry instruments to measure air pressure, humidity, and temperature. They have a radio transmitter to send the data back to Earth.

The lower atmosphere

The **atmosphere** is divided into layers. The lower atmosphere has two layers. The layer closest to the earth's surface is called the troposphere. It goes up to about 6 miles (10 kilometers). Most of the earth's weather happens in this layer.

The stratosphere is the next layer up. It goes from about 6 miles (10 kilometers) to about 31 miles (50 kilometers) above the earth's surface. This layer contains a lot of **ozone**. The ozone in this layer protects living things from the Sun's harmful rays. These rays cause sunburn and skin cancer. Without ozone, the Sun's rays could kill most living things on the earth.

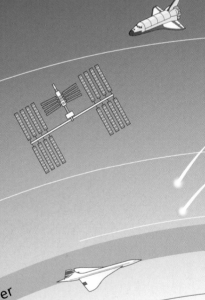

Outer space

1243 mi
(2000 km)

Exosphere

310 mi
(500 km)

Thermosphere

53 mi
(85 km)
Mesosphere

31 mi
(50 km)
Ozone layer

Stratosphere

6 mi
(10 km)

Troposphere

Word Bank

friction rubbing of one type of matter against another, causing heat
helium   gas that is lighter than air

The upper atmosphere

The upper atmosphere has three layers. The mesosphere goes from about 31 miles (50 kilometers) to about 53 miles (85 kilometers) above the earth. This layer has the coldest temperatures. It is also where meteors burn up because of **friction.** You see the burning meteors as shooting stars.

The thermosphere goes from about 53 miles (85 kilometers) to about 310 miles (500 kilometers) above the earth. Temperatures in this layer are very high. Because of the high temperatures, the gases in this layer break up into electrically charged **particles** called **ions.** So part of the thermosphere is called the ionosphere. This layer can reflect radio waves and makes long-distance communication possible. The international space station orbits in this layer.

The outermost layer is the exosphere. It contains very few particles. It extends from about 310 miles (500 kilometers) above the earth's surface to where outer space begins.

The space shuttle orbits the earth between 200 and 390 miles (322 and 620 kilometers) above the earth's surface. The shuttle's wings are useless in these parts of the atmosphere because there is so little air. The shuttle uses small bursts of power from rockets to move around.

Jet planes fly in the lower parts of the stratosphere.

Mount Everest

---

ion   atom or group of atoms with an electric charge
ozone   form of oxygen that absorbs harmful rays from the Sun

Plasmas

Sky flashes

Lightning is a giant spark of electricity. Lightning can travel between two clouds or from a cloud to the ground. A bolt of lightning passing through the air heats the gases. The air can become hotter than 48,000 °F (26,640 °C), turning its gases to plasma.

Atoms move faster as **matter** is heated. The faster the atoms move the greater the **force** with which they bump into other atoms. At very high temperatures, these collisions are violent. The atoms break up into the tiny **particles** that make them up. These tiny particles have electric charges. This new **state of matter** is called **plasma.** If gases are heated enough, they can become plasmas.

Fast Fact

The state of matter called plasma is different from the part of blood that is also called plasma. Blood plasma is a dense liquid.

The small dark spots in the Cat's Eye Nebula are clumps of dust and gas that are beginning to form stars.

Word Bank   nebula   cloud of dust and gas in outer space
nuclear fusion   reaction that takes place in stars, releasing energy

Where they are found

Plasmas are not common on the earth. But plasma is the most common state of matter in the universe. The space between the stars is not empty. It contains a lot of gas and dust. A huge cloud of gas and dust is called a **nebula**. Stars form within nebulas. As matter in a nebula clumps together, it gets hotter. Particles in the gas become plasma. When the temperature rises to several million degrees, **nuclear fusion** begins and a star is born. All stars, including the Sun, are glowing balls of plasma. Our Sun contains 99 percent of all the matter in our **solar system**. So plasma is also the most common form of matter in our solar system.

Plasma lights

This neon light glows red.

Fluorescent and neon lights are glass tubes filled with gases. When the lights are turned on, electricity flows through the tube. The electricity provides the energy that changes the gases into glowing plasma inside the tubes. The color depends on what kind of gas is inside.

---

plasma   gaslike mixture of charged particles at a high temperature
solar system   star and all the objects that orbit it

Changes in State

Molten mountain

When a volcano erupts, it sends out liquid rock from deep within the earth. This molten rock is called **lava**. Lava has temperatures between 1,560 °F (850 °C) and 2,280 °F (1,250 °C). As lava cools, it changes state. The liquid rock freezes and becomes solid.

The state of a substance depends on its temperature. If a liquid is cooled enough, it will change to a solid. This process is called **freezing.** If you fill an ice-cube tray with water and place it in a freezer, the water will turn to ice.

As a liquid cools, its **atoms** move closer together. Finally the atoms get so close that they form a solid. The temperature at which a liquid freezes is its **freezing point.** The freezing point of water is 32 °F (0 °C). The freezing point of mercury is −38 °F (−39 °C). That is why mercury has been used in outdoor thermometers.

A substance does not have to be cold to freeze. Many things change from liquid to solid at high temperatures. For example, aluminum freezes at 1,220 °F (660 °C).

The very runny lava that flows from Kilauea volcano in Hawaii is called pahoehoe. It can travel long distances before freezing into solid rock.

Word Bank　　freezing point　temperature at which a substance changes from liquid to solid

Melting

If a solid is heated, its atoms begin to move faster and farther apart. Finally the atoms are able to move around each other. The solid changes to a liquid. This process is called **melting.** Melting is the opposite of freezing. The temperature at which a solid changes to a liquid is its **melting point.** Ice melts at 32 °F (0 °C). Notice that the melting and freezing point of water are the same temperature. This is true for all substances. The melting point of aluminum is 1,220 °F (660 °C).

Melting and freezing points can help identify substances. If a sample of clear liquid does not freeze until its temperature is −144 °F (−98 °C), it isn't water.

Using pressure to melt ice

Melting and freezing points change with **pressure.** When a skater's metal blade presses on ice, the melting point is lowered. The ice melts. But when the skater moves on, the ice freezes again. Hockey players can move across the rink easily and quickly because of the coating of water under their skate blades.

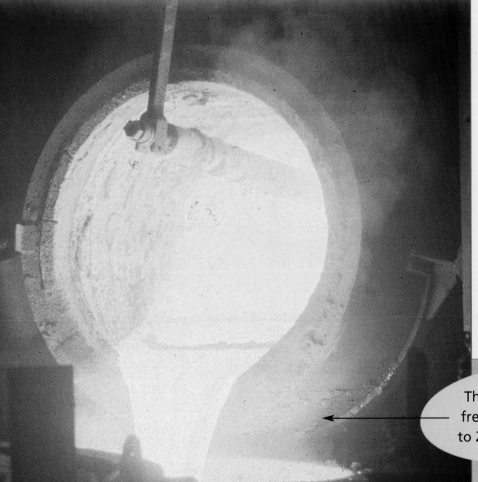

This liquid iron will freeze when it cools to 2,795 °F (1,535 °C).

---

melting point temperature at which a substance changes from solid to liquid

Skip the Liquid

A solid can change directly into a gas (**sublimation**) and a gas sometimes changes directly into a solid (**deposition**). These changes skip the liquid state. Frost is sublimation of water vapor in the air into ice **crystals**.

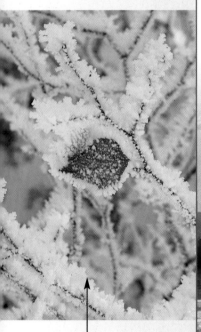

Ice crystals form directly from water vapor in cold air.

Evaporation

Puddles on the pavement disappear slowly as **particles** at the surface of the water gain enough energy to change to a gas. **Evaporation** is the gradual change from a liquid to a gas at the surface of a liquid. At any temperature, some **atoms** in a liquid move faster than others do. The fastest atoms escape from the liquid. In this way, water evaporates little by little.

Boiling

If a liquid is heated enough, it will change to a gas more quickly. The atoms move so fast that they constantly form bubbles of gas under the liquid's surface. The gas rises to the surface and escapes. This process is called **boiling.** Water boils at 212 °F (100 °C). This temperature is the **boiling point** of water. The boiling point of a substance is another **property** that can help us to identify it.

boiling point   temperature at which a liquid rapidly changes to a gas
deposition   changing from a gas state directly to a solid state

Condensation

A bathroom mirror might have drops of water on it after someone takes a hot shower. On some mornings the grass is wet even though it did not rain during the night. The reason for this is that water particles in the air cooled. As they cooled, the particles slowed down and moved closer together. Eventually, they changed from a gas to a liquid. This is called **condensation**. Condensation of water happens when warm, moist air cools. **Water vapor** condenses and forms water droplets on the cold bathroom mirror or when it comes into contact with cold grass. Usually, a gas will condense when it is cooled to its boiling point or below. Condensation is the opposite of evaporation and boiling.

Vapor lock is one of the most common causes of breakdowns in hot weather.

In hot weather, gasoline can **vaporize** in a car's fuel tank. This partly fills the fuel tank with gas rather than liquid. A car's fuel pump is designed to pump liquid, not gas. So the gasoline will not reach the car's engine and the car will not run.

Water evaporates from this hot spring. When the water vapor comes into contact with the cold air, it condenses into tiny droplets that we see as steam.

sublimation   changing from a solid state directly to a gas state
vaporize   to change from a liquid to a gas

Fluids in Action

Liquids and gases differ from solids because they flow. Any material that flows is called a **fluid**. Both liquids and gases are fluids that exert **pressure** on surfaces they touch.

Float or sink

About 2,200 years ago, a Greek scientist called Archimedes noticed that when an object is placed in water, it seems to weigh less. This is because the water pushes upward on the object. This upward **force** is the **buoyant force**. An object will float if the buoyant force is greater than the weight of the object. An object will sink if the buoyant force is less than the weight of the object. Ships float in water and hot air balloons float in air because of the buoyant force.

Scuba divers wear vests that can be inflated or deflated to make them rise or sink in the water.

Fish and divers

Most fish have an organ called a swim bladder. It controls their **buoyancy** in water. If they **inflate** the bladder, they rise in the water. If they **deflate** the bladder, they drop lower in the water. Scuba divers borrowed this idea.

Word Bank   buoyancy   ability to float
buoyant force   upward push of a fluid on any object placed in it

Transmitting fluid pressure

If you squeeze a plastic bottle with the lid on, the water has nowhere to go. The pressure in the water increases by the same amount everywhere in the container. It does not increase only where the bottle is squeezed or near the top of the bottle. When a force is applied to a contained fluid, the increase in pressure is transmitted to all parts of the fluid.

When a closed container of fluid has a hole in it, squeezing the container will force the fluid out of the hole. This is how we squeeze toothpaste out of a tube or ketchup from a plastic container. This arrangement is called a force pump.

Living force pumps

The human heart has two force pumps. One pump pushes blood from the right side of the heart to the lungs. In the lungs, the blood picks up oxygen and carries it back to the left side of the heart. The force pump on the left side of the heart pushes the blood to the rest of the body.

A hollow object like a ship floats if its total weight divided by its total **volume** is less than the **density** of water.

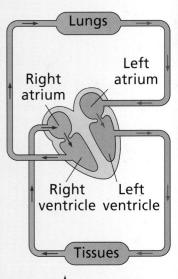

This is how the heart pumps blood around the body. Each pump has two parts— an atrium and a ventricle.

---

fluid   any matter that flows. Liquids and gases are fluids.

Breaking up concrete

A **pneumatic** drill is powered by air under pressure. Air is squeezed and travels through a hose to the drill. When the worker pulls the trigger, air pushes on a cylinder above a cutter. The cutter moves down and shatters the concrete. Then a valve opens and **compressed** air forces the cutter back up.

Hydraulics

Mechanics use a machine called a **hydraulic** jack when a car needs to have its tires changed. The lift has two cylinders. One cylinder is large and the other is small. A tank filled with **fluid** connects the two cylinders. Each cylinder has a **piston** at the top of the fluid level. Suppose a small **force** is applied to the small piston. The **pressure** on both pistons is increased by the same amount. But force is equal to **pressure** times the **area** of the piston. So a larger force is exerted on the large piston. In this way, a small force can raise a heavy car.

A hydraulic jack lets a person lift a car easily.

　　hydraulic　system operated by pressure transfer in a fluid

Fluid speed and pressure

In the 1700s Daniel Bernoulli discovered how the speed of fluids is related to pressure. The faster a fluid flows, the less pressure it exerts. This explains how airplanes can fly. Airplane wings have curved surfaces on the top, but the bottom is flat. As a plane moves forward, air passing over the wings has to travel farther than air passing under the wings. To take the same time to reach the back of the wing, air flows faster over the wing than it does under it. So the air pressure on the top of the wing is less than the air pressure under the wing. The greater upward pressure allows the plane to lift off the ground and fly.

Hydraulic jacks make use of the properties of fluids. A small force creates pressure that is transmitted through the fluid and pushes on the bigger piston. Because there is more area of this pressure to push on, a bigger force is created.

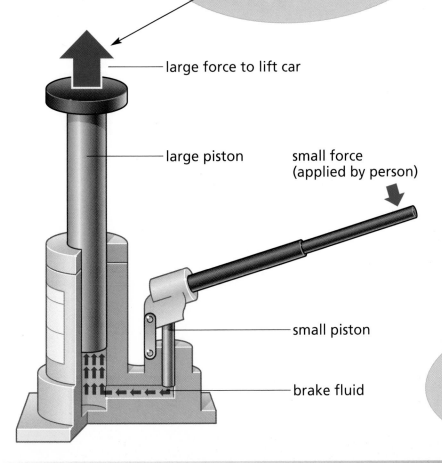

large force to lift car

large piston

small force (applied by person)

small piston

brake fluid

Windy cities

Fluids flow faster when they are forced through narrow spaces. In cities, wind is often forced to flow between rows of tall buildings. The reduced pressure outside the buildings sometimes means that the higher pressure inside the buildings blows out the windows.

The pressure caused by very strong winds shattered the windows of this Chicago skyscraper.

piston   metal cylinder that fits closely inside a tube; part of car engines and other machines

Weird Water

Water heats and cools slowly

Heated water takes a long time to cool off. It also takes a lot of heat to make cold water hot. That is why places near the ocean do not get as hot or as cold as places that are farther away from the water.

People often visit beaches in hot weather because it is cooler there.

Water is the only natural substance that we find in all three **states of matter** at temperatures normally found on the earth. Water can be found as ice, liquid water, and **water vapor.**

Water in its solid state can be found as:
- snow, **sleet,** and hail;
- ice on lakes, ponds, rivers, and streams;
- ice caps and **glaciers.**

Water in its liquid state can be found in:
- oceans;
- rivers and streams;
- lakes and ponds;
- swamps, marshes, and other wetlands;
- living things.

Water in its gas state can be found in:
- the **atmosphere.**

Just as ice cubes float in a cold drink, an iceberg floats in the ocean. But only about 10 percent of the iceberg is above the water. The part under the water that cannot be seen is nine times as large.

Word Bank glacier large mass of snow and ice that moves slowly

Ice floats

The solid state of most substances is much denser that the liquid state. So solid iron would sink in liquid iron. But water is unusual. The solid state is less dense than the liquid. So ice floats. Like most substances, water **contracts** as it cools. But once it has cooled below 39 °F (4 °C), it starts to **expand** again. As it continues to cool and expand, a lot of empty spaces form between its **particles.** When it reaches 32 °F (0 °C), the expanded liquid **freezes** and becomes ice.

It is a good thing that water does this. The top layer of a body of water freezes first. If this ice sank, more ice would continue to form on the surface and this, too, would sink. More lakes and ponds would freeze solid in winter, killing many living things in the water.

Water in living things

The largest jellyfish is the Lion's Mane. It can reach 8 feet (2.5 meters) across with tentacles 197 feet (60 meters) long.

All living things contain water. Jellyfish are over 90 percent water. Up to 60 percent of the human body is water. The brain is about 70 percent water. Blood is about 82 percent water. And the lungs are nearly 90 percent water.

Groundwater

One of the most important sources of freshwater is **groundwater**. The earth has about 30 times more groundwater than freshwater in lakes and rivers. To use most groundwater, people have to drill wells and pump the water to the surface.

This drilling rig can drill water wells deep into solid rock.

Earth's water

Water covers about 75 percent of the earth's surface. Most of this water, about 97 percent, is in the oceans. We cannot drink this salty water or use it for washing. We cannot use it to grow crops or to operate electrical power plants, either. We need freshwater for these things. Freshwater contains few minerals. But only about three percent of the earth's water is fresh.

Where is the freshwater?

About 66 percent of the freshwater on the earth is frozen as ice. It is locked up in **glaciers** in Antarctica, in Greenland and on high mountains. People cannot use it. Less than one percent of the earth's water is useable, liquid, freshwater.

Fast Fact
The same water that existed on the earth millions of years ago is still here. The water you drink today could have been drunk by a dinosaur more than 65 million years ago.

Word Bank   glacier   large mass of snow and ice that moves slowly
groundwater   water collected in tiny spaces underground

The water cycle

Water on the earth is constantly changing and moving from place to place. The changing and movement of water is called the **water cycle.** The energy that runs the water cycle comes from the Sun. This energy **evaporates** water from oceans, lakes, and rivers. The **water vapor** rises into the **atmosphere** where it cools. The water vapor **condenses**, changing from a gas to a liquid, and forms clouds. Tiny droplets inside clouds join to form bigger drops. Finally, they fall as rain, snow, **sleet,** or hail. Rain or **melted** ice runs off the land into streams and rivers. Then water flows into lakes and oceans and so the cycle continues.

Plants are part of the water cycle

condensation

evaporation

rain, snow, or hail

heated by the Sun

water runs off land into oceans

Plants need water in order to live and grow. Their roots take in water from the ground. Plants also give off water vapor through their leaves. This process adds water vapor to the atmosphere and is called **transpiration.**

The earth's water continually cycles between the oceans, land, and atmosphere.

transpiration   process in which plants give off water vapor from leaves
water cycle   continuous cycle of water on the earth

Further Information

Organizations

Science Made Simple

Learn about science "hands on." Site includes science news, projects, facts, more.
sciencemadesimple.com

Rader Studios

Fun science news, plus activities including quizzes, experiments, tutorials, and more.
chem4kids.com

Lawrence Livermore National Laboratory

Get science news from a national security laboratory.
llnl.gov

Books

Greenaway, Theresa. *The Water Cycle.* Chicago: Raintree, 2001.

Hunter, Rebecca. *Discovering Science: Matter.* Chicago: Raintree, 2003.

Snedden, Robert. *Material World: States of Matter.* Chicago: Heinemann, 2001.

World Wide Web

If you want to find out more about **states of matter,** you can search the Internet using keywords like these:

- "states of matter" OR "phases of matter"
- solids + liquids + gases
- plasma + state
- "water cycle"
- "Earth's atmosphere"
- water + evaporation + condensation
- hydraulics + science

You can also find your own keywords by using headings or words from this book. Use the search tips below to help you find the most useful websites.

Search tips

There are billions of pages on the Internet so it can be difficult to find exactly what you are looking for. For example, if you just type in "water" on a search engine like Google, you will get a list of 85 million web pages. These search skills will help you find useful websites more quickly:

- Know exactly what you want to find out about first.
- Use simple keywords instead of whole sentences.
- Use two to six keywords in a search, putting the most important words first.
- Be precise—only use names of people, places, or things.
- If you want to find words that go together, put quote marks around them, for example, "states of matter."
- Use the advanced section of your search engine.
- Use the + sign to add certain words to your search.

Where to search

Search engine

A search engine looks through the entire web and lists all the sites that match the words in the search box. It can give thousands of links, but the best matches are at the top of the list, on the first page. Try **google.com**

Search directory

A search directory is more like a library of websites that have been sorted by a person instead of a computer. You can search by keyword or subject and browse through the different sites in the same way you would look through books on a library shelf. A good example is **yahooligans.com**

Glossary

acid chemical that contains hydrogen and has a pH of less than 7

altitude distance above the ocean (sea level)

amorphous solid in which particles are not arranged in an orderly pattern

area amount of surface, measured in square inches or square feet

atmosphere layer of gases that surround a planet like the earth

atom smallest particle of an element

boil rapid change of state from a liquid to a gas that takes place within the liquid as well as at its surface

boiling point temperature at which a liquid rapidly changes to a gas

buoyancy ability to float

buoyant force upward push of a fluid on any object placed in it

composite material designed by combining other materials with properties that go well together

compress to squeeze into a smaller space

condensation process of changing from a gas to a liquid

conduction transfer of heat or electricity from one particle to another in a solid

conductor material through which heat or electricity passes easily

contract to become smaller in size; take up less space

convection flow of heat due to the rise of hotter matter in liquid or gas

crystal solid in which particles are arranged in an orderly, repeating pattern

deflate to let air or gas out of an object

density amount of mass in a certain volume of matter

deposition change from a gas state directly to a solid state

diffuse how particles of a gas spread evenly through another gas

digest break food down so it can be used by the body

esophagus pipe from the mouth to the stomach

evaporation process of changing from a liquid to a gas at the surface of the liquid

expand to become larger in size; to take up more space

flexible able to stretch or bend

fluid any matter that flows. Liquids and gases are fluids.

force push or pull

freeze to change from a liquid to a solid

freezing point temperature at which a substance changes from a liquid to a solid

friction rubbing of one type of mattter against another, causing heat

geothermal energy heat from deep inside the earth

geyser vent that shoots hot water and steam from underground

glacier large mass of snow and ice that moves slowly

groundwater water collected in tiny spaces underground

helium gas that is lighter than air

humid moist or damp

hydraulic system operated by pressure transfer through a fluid

inflate to force air or gas into an object

insulate to stop from conducting heat or electricity

ion atom or group of atoms with an electric charge

keyword word that sums up a topic

lava molten rock that has risen to the earth's surface

lubricate make slippery; reduce friction

mass amount of matter in an object

matter anything that takes up space and has weight

melt change from a solid to a liquid

melting point temperature at which a substance changes from a solid to a liquid

meteorite lump of space rock or metal that has crashed into a planet

nebula cloud of dust and gas in outer space

nuclear fusion reaction that takes place in the stars, releasing energy

odor smell

odorless without any smell

ozone form of oxygen that absorbs harmful rays from the Sun

particle tiny piece

physical change change in how something looks or acts, not in what makes it up

piston metal cylinder that fits closely inside a tube; part of car engines and other machines

plasma gaslike mixture of charged particles at a high temperature

pneumatic powered by high-pressure air

pressure force divided by the area it presses on, measured in newtons per square foot (newtons per square meter)

property feature of something

recycled treated so that the material can be used again

shale rock formed from clay or mud in thin layers

sleet mixture of rain and snow

solar system star and all the objects that orbit it

state of matter whether something is solid, liquid, or gas

sublimation change from a solid state directly to a gas state

suitable right for the job

surface tension force that pulls atoms of a liquid together at its surface

transpiration process in which plants give off water vapor from their leaves

vaporize to change from a liquid to a gas

viscosity how easily a liquid flows or pours

volume amount of space that something takes up

water cycle continuous cycle of water on the earth

water vapor water in gas form

Index